ROBIN HOOD

RETOLD BY SARAH HAYES

ILLUSTRATED BY PATRICK BENSON

WALKER BOOKS
LONDON

AUTHOR'S NOTE

No one knows exactly when Robin Hood lived. He is a figure from legend, not history. Most of the stories told here are taken from a collection of popular ballads printed in 1495, but they tell of a hero from a much earlier time. I have chosen to set this book at the end of the twelfth century during the reign of Richard I and to make Robin the son of a farmer, not the nobleman suggested by writers of more recent times.

First published 1989 by
Walker Books Ltd, 87 Vauxhall Walk
London SE11 5HJ

Text © 1989 Sarah Hayes
Illustrations © 1989 Patrick Benson

First printed 1989
Printed and bound by Butler & Tanner, Frome

British Library Cataloguing in Publication Data
Hayes, Sarah
Robin Hood.—
I. Title
II. Benson, Patrick
823'.914 [J]   PZ8.1

ISBN 0-7445-0746-4

CONTENTS

TRAPPED

ROBERT STOPPED and whistled quietly to his dog. The dog froze. Not ten paces away a hind and fawn were drinking from the stream. A twig crackled in the undergrowth and the hind lifted her head. For a moment she looked at Robert. He was a tall, slightly built young man, with clear grey eyes and a cheerful grin. As the deer turned to run, Robert heard the unmistakable sound of a bowstring. An arrow whistled out of the trees behind him. The deer staggered and then fell.

Robert was horrified. "Only cowards shoot hinds and fawns!" he shouted. "Come out of the forest and show yourself, coward!" In the next moment he felt his arm pinned behind his back. As he struggled, another man rushed out of the bushes and seized his bow. "Robert Locksley," he said, "you are charged with killing the King's deer. You will be taken before the Sheriff and sentenced to death."

"The hind had a young fawn," said Robert indignantly. "I could never have shot her!"

"But you did," said a cold voice. A man on a black horse rode forward and stood over him. "There are witnesses."

Robert looked up and recognised the thin face and deep-set eyes of Sir Guy of Gisborne. He realised that he had been trapped. Sir Guy and his men must have tracked him into the forest and waited for the right moment.

"The Sheriff takes an interest in poachers," said Sir Guy, "especially those like you who have been heard to speak ill of our noble lord, Prince John."

"That cut-throat," Robert muttered.

"As I expected, a traitor as well as a poacher," Sir Guy said smoothly. "Prince John will be so pleased to hear of your death."

Robert watched the motherless fawn run into the forest. If only he could escape so easily. He knew that Sir Guy and the Sheriff of Nottingham wished him dead. Sir Guy had long wanted to get his hands on Locksley Farm. And the Sheriff had orders to kill anyone who breathed a word against Prince John. It was high time King Richard returned from fighting the Saracens, thought Robert. England had become an evil place in his absence.

Two mail-clad men bound Robert's hands and attached them to a long rope. Sir Guy tied the rope to his saddle and kicked his horse into a fast trot. Half running, half stumbling along at the end of the rope, Robert felt like a dancing bear. He looked up at the canopy of leaves and wondered whether he would ever see the great oaks of Sherwood Forest again.

As the path widened into a clearing, an owl hooted from a tree on the right. Another called from the left. Strange to hear owls in the middle of the day, thought Robert. Then it happened. Two figures leapt down from an enormous oak and pulled Sir Guy off his horse. A little man ran forward and seized Sir Guy's sword. Ten more men surrounded the mail-clad soldiers. Robert had heard people speak of forest robbers, but he had never seen them before. They looked a fierce and unkempt bunch.

A tall man came forward. He was dressed in a faded russet uniform. With one slash of his sword, he cut the leather purse from Sir Guy's belt. As he raised his sword again, Robert shouted, "Stop! You have what you want. There is no need to kill him."

The tall man whirled round. "Who are you to give the orders?" he said.

Robert answered him with a question. "Who are you to kill an unarmed man?"

The tall man hesitated. There was something about the young man's open face and serious grey eyes that made him feel ashamed. He sheathed his sword, and left Sir

Guy of Gisborne moaning on the ground. Then he murmured something to the little man, who vanished into the forest still waving Sir Guy's sword.

"Jack and Ned, stay behind," the tall man ordered. He unfastened the rope from the black horse's saddle. "As for this bearcub, he shall come with us." He gave a sudden pull on the rope and Robert lost his balance. "Can you do any other tricks, cub?" he asked and laughed. Then, as silently as they had come, all but two of the robbers melted back into the forest. And Robert Locksley went with them.

Half an hour later, however, the little man returned with several coils of rope, and Sir Guy and his soldiers were made ready for their return journey. The forest robbers were well pleased with their handiwork, but Sir Guy did not look happy as he rode into Nottingham. He stared straight ahead and pretended not to notice the gasps of stifled laughter which followed him through the town and up to the gates of the Sheriff's castle.

THE SHERIFF'S PRESENT

IN THE LATE afternoon the Sheriff of Nottingham sat alone at his table. It was not a cold day, but the Sheriff was wearing several layers of clothing and a short fur-trimmed cape. He was a little fat man who always felt the cold. Even now a huge fire blazed in the hearth.

The Sheriff was annoyed. Sir Guy was late and he had been forced to eat alone. The stuffed peacocks had been very good, but he had eaten too many of them. The Sheriff picked his teeth and his servants waited for him to shout at them.

Everyone heard the gates clang in the courtyard below. The Sheriff stood up. Gisborne was here at last! And if all had gone well, that fellow Locksley would now be his prisoner. The Sheriff could hear shouting and laughing in the courtyard. He hurried over to the window and looked out. He had to stand on tiptoe to see into the courtyard, and for a moment he did not believe the scene which met his eyes. He blinked and looked again.

Below him stumbled a little procession of exhausted men and horses. Sir Guy and one of his men had been tied back to back and set on Sir Guy's black charger. The horse hung its head and dragged its feet as if ashamed of its burden. The other soldiers had been roped together in a line to follow along behind, and a little pack-pony completed the cavalcade.

The Sheriff was beside himself with rage. He flew down the stone steps into the courtyard. "What is the meaning of this?" he shrieked. Sir Guy did not reply, but the Sheriff could read his answer on the parchment pinned to the pack-pony's saddle-cloth:

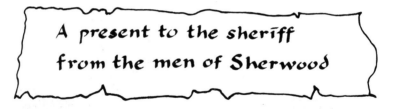

A present to the sheriff
from the men of Sherwood

"What does it mean?" he shouted. "Who are the men of Sherwood? And where is Locksley? What does it mean?" he repeated.

"It means," said Sir Guy slowly, "that Robert Locksley is taken."

"Taken!" shrieked the Sheriff. "Taken where?"

"Taken by forest robbers," replied Sir Guy.

"Is he dead?" asked the Sheriff eagerly. "Are we rid of him at last?"

Sir Guy nodded. He did not know for certain that Locksley was dead, but the tall robber looked a murderous fellow. Young Locksley would be dead before nightfall, he was sure.

The Sheriff began to feel more cheerful. He was not fond of Sir Guy, but the man had proved useful to him on more than one occasion. "You are late for dinner, Gisborne," he said testily. But Sir Guy was beyond caring. As a servant loosened his bonds, he slipped down from his horse and fell to the ground in a faint.

THE GREENWOOD

TWELVE MILES from Nottingham, in the heart of Sherwood Forest, a young man with keen grey eyes sat beside a roaring fire. Robert Locksley was very much alive. The robbers had untied his hands as soon as they had reached their camp, and given him a fine supper. Now they wanted to know all about the young man who had dared to defy their leader – the tall man they called Will Scarlet.

"There is little to tell," said Robert. "Locksley Farm came to me from my father, and his father before him. Now it is in the hands of Sir Guy of Gisborne; and I am an outlaw, like yourselves."

"We are proud to call ourselves outlaws," Will said quietly, "for much wickedness is done in the name of the law these days."

"Death to Prince John!" shouted a black-bearded man from the circle round the fire.

"Death to the Sheriff!" roared someone else. Then everyone began shouting together until the tall man held up his hand. He turned to Robert. "We are for the King," he said.

"And I," said Robert simply. "May he soon return."

The tall man again held up his hand. "We men of Sherwood have been forced to leave our homes and families, to choose a new way of life here in the forest –"

"And kill innocent travellers for gold?" interrupted Robert.

Will tried to explain. "We take only from those who have stolen from others," he said.

"And end up thieves and murderers," Robert added.

"They are all brave men," said Will. But the outlaws were silent. The young man made them feel uncomfortable.

Robert broke the silence. "I have seen the faces of the poor," he said. "They are not free like you. They are tied forever to cruel masters like Sir Guy of Gisborne. The little they have is taken from them by the men of power."

"By the Sheriff, more like," someone said.

"Aye, and that fat Abbot at St Mary's," added the little man.

"Quiet, Much," said Will. He was listening intently.

"Steal from the rich, by all means," continued Robert, "they have more than enough. But why not give back to the poor what has been taken from them?"

"Rob the rich to feed the poor," said the black-bearded man, "is that what you mean?"

"I think so," said Robert in some confusion. He had not meant to give a speech.

"Will you join us here in the forest?" asked Will suddenly.

Robert laughed. "I think I have no choice," he answered. "But I have much to learn."

"First you should have a new name," said Will. Then he smiled. "You must forgive the rough treatment in the forest: with any luck the Sheriff thinks you dead by now. He must not hear the name of Locksley again." He looked down at his suit of faded russet, and added, "I was not born to the name of Will Scarlet."

"Nor I Jack Smithy," said the man with the beard.

"They call me Much the Miller," said the little man.

Will looked at Robert. "What do you say to Robin O' Greenwood?" he asked.

"Too long," muttered Jack Smithy.

"Robin Wood?" suggested Robert.

"We have a Wood already," a new voice said. "Thomas Wood of Dale."

Robert pulled his cloak over his head and grinned. "Shall it be Robin Hood, then?"

"Aye," said Will, "Robin Hood will do."

"Robin Hood is good," said Jack Smithy, who was somewhat too fond of the sound of his own voice. "But what can Robin Hood give us in return for his new name? He looks hardly more than a boy."

"I can plough a straight furrow," said Robin.

"In the forest!" said Jack in disgust.

"I can tell a good cow."

"Deer are the only beasts in Sherwood," Jack growled.

"I can use a bow," said Robin. "My father taught me."

"Not so well as Will, I'll bet," said someone.

The tall man stepped into the firelight. "I am glad to meet a fellow archer," he said. "Tomorrow we shall test your skill."

The robbers were impatient. "The wand, the wand," they shouted. "Let us have the contest now." Robin's father had told him about the wand. It was a whippy length of peeled willow nailed to a tree, almost impossible to hit in broad daylight. Now night was falling fast.

"Jack found your bow in the forest," said Will, and the black-bearded man handed Robin his beloved silver-tipped bow. Robin peered into the gloom. The wand was barely visible. He took aim and shot. His arrow landed a finger's breadth from the wand. Will's arrow landed quivering between Robin's and the wand. The robbers roared their approval. Robin took a deep breath and shot again. This time the arrow flew straight to the wand and split it clean in two. The robbers gasped.

"Not bad for a farmer's boy," said Jack.

Will bowed. "I have never split the wand," he said.

"Nor had I before this moment," said Robin. He had surprised himself.

In the months that followed, the outlaws taught Robin everything they knew. He learned how to walk silently in the forest paths, how to hoot like an owl and how to wait for hours in the rain wedged in the fork of a tree. He learned how to fight with knives, how to wrestle, and how to tell a good story.

Robin felt that he had little to offer in return: a keen eye and a sure aim, that was all. But he was wrong. The outlaws found in Robin something that had been missing from their lives. The young man's enthusiasm, his sense of fun and his gentle ways reminded them of the homes and families they had lost. Soon Robin became the undisputed leader of the band.

Within a year over a hundred men had come to Sherwood. They were no longer a dirty, dishevelled band of robbers but a highly trained army, dressed in Lincoln green and dedicated to Robin's rallying call – rob the rich to feed the poor. Many a starving peasant had his grain sack mysteriously filled, and hungry families found food waiting on their doorsteps. People began to talk with awe about Robin Hood and the men of Sherwood. But while the poor folk rejoiced, the rich grew angry. Two men in particular feared and hated the name of Robin Hood – a cold-voiced knight and a little fat man with a gold chain – Sir Guy of Gisborne and the Sheriff of Nottingham.

THE FIGHT ON THE BRIDGE

WHEN THE SUN shone and no travellers were reported, the outlaws would often hunt in the forest. One winter's day Robin found himself on the wrong side of a fast-flowing stream, separated from the rest of the hunting party. He knew he would have to make for the old bridge half a mile away.

But when he reached the bridge, Robin stopped. On the far side of the stream stood the biggest man he had ever seen. "A giant," he gasped, and he made the sign of the cross. But the man was human enough. He stood motionless, rooted like a great tree. "Allow me to cross the bridge, fair stranger," shouted Robin. "You are blocking my path."

The giant shook his mane of tangled yellow hair. He put one foot on the bridge. "I was here first!" he shouted.

By way of answer Robin loosed off an arrow which landed neatly in the giant's hat.

"A feather for your cap!" said Robin.

The giant plucked out the arrow and threw it into the stream. Then he turned his staff across his body and strode to the centre of the bridge. "Do you still wish to cross?" he roared.

Robin ran to a nearby clump of hazel and cut himself a staff. "Yes," he shouted, "I still wish to cross." Then he rushed to the centre of the bridge and delivered such a blow to the giant's knees that his hands ached. The giant did not even blink. Then the fight began in earnest. The forest rang with the sound of staff on staff, as each parried the other's blows. The giant was stronger and more skilled with the staff. But Robin was quicker on his feet. At last Robin leapt on to the parapet of the bridge. Now he had the advantage. The giant's back was turned towards him, unprotected. Robin raised his staff to deliver the final blow, but the huge stranger seemed to have eyes in the back of his head.

"So that's the way of it, little man!" he shouted, and with a quick backwards jab he thrust his staff into Robin's ribs. Robin lost his balance, teetered on the parapet and fell, spluttering as he hit the cold water of the stream. Then he disappeared. The giant looked about him: the current was strong and the water treacherous. He had meant only to teach the little fighting cock a lesson, not to drown him. He knelt down and looked into the foaming water.

From under the bridge came three clear calls of a hunting horn. Then Robin, who had been clinging to the bridge, splashed his way to the bank and pulled himself out. Robin's dog barked with excitement as Will Scarlet and ten men rushed out of the forest and took hold of the giant.

"Robin, are you hurt?" shouted Will.

"No," said Robin, "just a little wet."

"Then this giant fellow shall be wetter still," shouted Jack Smithy. He and four others lifted up the huge man and would have hurled him into the deepest part of the stream had not Robin held up his hand.

"No! The man fought fair and won fair."

"Robin Hood worsted in a fight!" said Will. "That is something new."

"So this is the famous Robin Hood," said the stranger slowly. "Defender of the poor."

"And scourge of the Sheriff," added Jack Smithy.

The giant's face darkened. "I have my own score to settle with the Sheriff," he said. Then he threw back his yellow mane and laughed. "Well, Master Fighting Cock, I shall teach you to use a quarterstaff, and you will teach me to use a bow. Is it a bargain?"

"It is," replied Robin. "But first you must tell us your name."

The huge man looked down. "My name is John," he said. "John Little."

The outlaws burst into a roar of laughter. "Henceforth you shall be known as Little John," cried Robin and he clapped the big man on the back. "Now we have Much the Miller who is little, and Little John who is much."

So it was that Little John came to Sherwood and fought a fair fight to become Robin's trusty right-hand man.

THE RESCUE

WITH LITTLE JOHN'S help Robin carried out daring raids far beyond the borders of Sherwood. The wealthy citizens of Nottingham were his chief victims. One spring a gathering of wool merchants had their purses cut from their belts while they sat at table. The following autumn a cruel justice found his money sacks filled with acorns and all his gold gone. No one recognised Robin as the stout serving-man or Little John as the wandering monk. But everyone knew the meaning of the arrow shot into the justice's courtyard. The people of Nottingham began to laugh at their Sheriff who seemed so helpless against the men of Sherwood.

The Sheriff grew angry. He decided to punish the people who dared to laugh at him. He trebled the taxes. He threw people into prison on the merest suspicion. He gave the death penalty for the smallest offence. Robin was horrified. He withdrew into the forest and kept away from Nottingham. But the list of people hanged and imprisoned grew longer.

One night an old woman stumbled into his camp. "Master Hood," she cried, "I seek Master Robin Hood."

"You have found him, lady," said Robin. He led the old woman to a seat by the fire.

"It is my grandsons," sobbed the old woman. "Three innocent young boys. The Sheriff has ordered them hanged at nine o'clock tomorrow morning."

"Your grandsons will not die, I promise you," said Robin firmly. "What was the boys' offence?" he asked.

"They took an egg," the old woman replied, "one small egg from a nest they found in Master Bolt's hay store."

Robin sighed: there would be no justice in England until King Richard returned. He smiled at the old woman. "You must be tired and hungry," he said. While the old woman ate and then slept, Robin, Little John, and Will Scarlet talked.

The next day, as a pale wintry sun rose over the outlaws' camp, the old woman sat staring into the fire. Two men stood guard under the great oak. Otherwise the camp was deserted.

It was market day in Nottingham and the town was already buzzing with activity. A platform had been built in the market square, and a gallows set upon it. Armed men lined the platform. A large crowd had gathered, but no one took any notice of the rosy-cheeked apple-woman who stood near the row of seats reserved for the Sheriff and his guests. All eyes were on the platform. Just before nine o'clock, a hush came over the crowd. Even the calves in their pens stopped bellowing for a moment. The small stout figure of the Sheriff bustled into his seat. He was followed by a thin-faced man clearly well-known to the crowd. "Sir Guy of Gisborne," the whisper ran. "And the Lady Marian Fitzwalter," added some. Sir Guy held the arm of a young girl, no more than seventeen years old. A stiff linen head-dress held back her hair, but a few unruly black curls had escaped.

The clock began to strike. Three boys, the youngest a child of nine or ten, were led out, bound and blindfolded. A drum beat a solemn tattoo.

The apple-woman reached into her basket and brought out a hunting horn. She blew the horn, loud and clear, and a hail of arrows landed on the platform. Several of the Sheriff's men fell, while others drew their bows and shot at random into the crowd. Sir Guy of Gisborne leapt out of his seat, his sword drawn.

The apple-woman ripped off her bulky skirts and jumped on to the platform. "Robin Hood!" the crowd shouted. A bent old man threw away his crutches, and straightened up. His great mane of yellow hair shone out over the heads of the crowd. "Little John!" All was confusion on the platform. The rain of arrows had stopped, and people were fighting hand to hand. The

Sheriff cowered in terror under the platform. Using his basket as a shield, Robin fought his way towards Sir Guy of Gisborne. Suddenly Sir Guy slipped backwards and fell into the jeering crowd. At the same moment Robin saw the black-haired girl move across to the three blindfolded boys standing beneath the gallows. She took a little dagger out of her sleeve and cut their bonds. Then she pushed them gently off the platform.

When he saw the boys disappear into the crowd, Robin jumped down. As he passed the Lady Marian, he whispered. "My thanks, lady, you have saved their lives." Then he added, "But I do not like your choice of escort."

"He is not my choice," whispered the Lady Marian fiercely. Then Robin was gone. The people of Nottingham had no love for the Sheriff and his cruel laws, and they let Robin through, closing in against the soldiers who tried to follow him.

Before the clock in the square struck the quarter hour, Robin and his band were clear of the town and heading back to Sherwood. A hundred and twenty outlaws had entered Nottingham that morning. Now their number was increased to a hundred and twenty-three, and an old woman had seen her grandsons saved from certain death.

MAID MARIAN

LORD FITZWALTER and Sir Guy of Gisborne were neighbours. Ten years ago Lady Marian Fitzwalter had been betrothed to Sir Guy. She had been seven years old then, and Sir Guy had not been kind to her. He would not let her ride on his horse and he never smiled.

"I would rather die than marry Sir Guy," she told her father.

"I shall lock you up," replied Lord Fitzwalter.

"I'll steal the key."

"I shall raise the drawbridge."

"Then I shall swim the moat!"

"I shall put you in the tower."

"I'll knot my clothes together and climb down!" said Lady Marian.

Lord Fitzwalter shook his head. His daughter was headstrong and wilful. She could swim and ride as well as any boy, and she could even use a sword. Her father sighed. He did not like Sir Guy but he owed him money. Sir Guy had agreed to cancel the debt as soon as the wedding had taken place. "You cannot keep him waiting any longer, Marian," Lord Fitzwalter said. "He is coming this evening to settle matters. I expect you to be polite."

Lady Marian angrily left the room.

When her servants came to dress their mistress for Sir Guy's visit, Lady Marian was nowhere to be found. "Hiding in the hayloft; I expect," said her old nurse, but she feared that her mistress might have gone much further afield.

Early the following day Robin Hood was walking on the edge of the forest when he came upon a boy sitting under a tree. Robin pulled up the hood of his cloak. The Sheriff had spies everywhere, even in Sherwood. "Don't you know there is danger in the forest," he said. "It is not a place for children."

"I am not a child," said the boy. "I have come to join Robin Hood."

"That rascal," said Robin.

"He is not a rascal!" shouted the boy, drawing his sword.

"I don't fight children," said Robin. But the boy was so angry that Robin feared for his life and drew his own sword. The two fought intently for a few minutes. Then the boy's blade scratched Robin's cheek. At the same moment Robin's sword caught the boy's sleeve. With

blood pouring down his cheek, Robin put down his sword and pushed back his hair. He heard the boy gasp.

"You are… you are…"

"That rascal, Robin Hood," said Robin. "And you?"

"Don't you recognise me?" said the boy and he took off his cap. The black curls tumbled down and it was Robin's turn to be surprised.

"The Lady Marian Fitzwalter!" he said. "But I have hurt you."

"It's only a scratch," said the Lady Marian airily. "Don't you think these clothes suit me?" Robin looked at the leather doublet and woollen hose. He had not forgotten the beautiful black-haired girl who had helped to rescue the three boys.

"But Sir Guy?" he said.

"I told my father I would rather die than marry him," said the Lady Marian. "Then I had a better idea."

"A better idea," echoed Robin.

"I thought I would run away and join Robin Hood. I can ride and I can fight."

"So I see," said Robin. "I ought to send you back to your father."

"Back to Sir Guy?" wailed Lady Marian. Her face was so pitiful that Robin laughed.

"You may stay in Sherwood on one condition."

"What is it?" the girl asked nervously.

"You are never to go anywhere near Nottingham again."

"Is that all?" said Lady Marian. "I never want to see Nottingham again, or Sir Guy, or that horrid little Sheriff."

Robin's men were doubtful about the new recruit. But the Lady Marian soon won all their hearts. It was Jack Smithy who first called her Maid Marian – "Fighting with swords is no work for a lady," he growled, but he had to admit that she was more than a match for him with the short sword. Soon no one remembered that Maid Marian had once been the Lady Marian Fitzwalter.

Before the year was out Robin and Marian were married, and the forest rang with sounds of feasting and merriment.

The Sheriff's spies brought him news of the wedding.

"So that rogue has married Lord Fitzwalter's daughter," he wheezed. Then he turned to Sir Guy. "And I thought she was promised to you, Gisborne." Sir Guy looked away and the Sheriff could not resist adding, "Too lively for you, was she?"

Sir Guy said nothing. But in his heart he swore to kill Robin Hood.

THREE WHISTLES

THE AUTUMN THAT followed Robin's wedding was wet. It rained and rained, and the river running through Sherwood burst its banks.

Robin wanted to go to St Mary's Abbey to the north of the forest, and that meant swimming across the flooded river. He was about to plunge into the water when he caught sight of someone sitting on a boulder, staring at the flood. He was a great fat fellow, as round as a turnip and dressed in the brown habit of a friar. Robin waved. The friar stood up and brandished the chicken leg he was holding. A huge sword was tucked into the rope tied round his habit. He was dripping wet.

Robin suspected a trick. The friar wore the cross of St Mary's, and the Abbot there was well known to be an old friend of the Sheriff. Robin drew his bow and aimed it at the friar.

"Good morning, brother," he said politely. "I find

myself on the wrong side of this flood. Would you be so kind as to carry me across since you are wet already?"

The friar lurched to his feet and threw down his chicken leg. He stood head and shoulders above Robin, but his black eyes twinkled merrily.

"Climb on my back, stranger," he said.

Robin slung his bow over his head, and with much splashing and puffing the friar carried him across the flooded river. As soon as they reached the bank, the friar put one huge arm round Robin's shoulders.

"Now I am on the wrong side," he said softly, and he tightened his grasp across Robin's back. "It is your turn to carry me across."

Robin's heart sank, but he braced himself as the huge man climbed on to his back. Very slowly the two made their way across the river. Once Robin missed his footing and staggered, but he did not fall. He could hardly speak when they reached the bank. "Now I am on the wrong side," he panted.

The fat friar solemnly lifted Robin on to his back and strode out into the middle of the stream. And there he dropped him, quite deliberately, into the deepest part of the river.

"So you want a fight," shouted Robin. He was out of the water in an instant, and the two men were soon wrestling on the muddy banks of the river. Like many fat men, the friar was quicker on his feet than he looked. The fight

went on and on. Robin began to think that it would never end. Eventually, covered in mud and barely able to move, he managed to find his horn and blow three blasts on it.

In a few minutes Maid Marian and a dozen men ran out of the tangled undergrowth. The friar let go his hold on Robin and drew out a silver whistle that hung round his neck. "If Robin Hood can summon help, so can I," he shouted. He blew three shrill blasts on the whistle. There was a noise of yelping and snarling and a pack of fierce fighting dogs streamed out of the forest. The outlaws shot arrow after arrow at them, but the dogs just dodged and darted about and caught the arrows in their teeth.

Robin crossed himself. "These are hounds from hell, friar," he said.

The fat man roared with laughter. "Just well trained beasts," he replied. He blew the whistle again and the dogs retreated to swirl round his feet, licking his hands and wagging their tails.

"It seems there is to be no winner in this fight," said Robin. "You have guessed my name, but tell me who you are, friar, for I shall not forget our first muddy meeting."

"Brother Michael Tuck, sometime of St Mary's Abbey."

"I was on my way to the abbey myself," said Robin. "Your Abbot is well acquainted with us."

Several times the outlaws had managed to ambush the Abbot in the forest on his way home from Nottingham.

He was a greedy man who cared more about a fine wine than a sick peasant. "But Brother Michael is far from St Mary's today," Robin continued.

"Not far enough," growled the friar. "Tomorrow I must go back – to sing at a wedding."

"A wedding is nothing to grumble about," said Robin. He smiled at Maid Marian.

Brother Michael frowned. "This one is. It should never take place. That Abbot of mine is forcing a young girl to marry a sack of bones old enough to be her grandfather. And all for the sake of a purse of silver pieces. I'm not going back. I shall stay here in the forest with you!"

"You can stay, Brother Michael, but not today," said Robin. "Tomorrow's wedding will have some uninvited guests and you must be there to welcome them."

Brother Michael grinned. "Uninvited guests," he repeated thoughtfully. Then his expression changed. "I shall go back to the abbey, if you say so, but only on one condition – that you give me a proper meal before I go!"

It was a very well-fed friar who made his way back to the abbey that evening. He chewed his crusts with the other monks, and did not cast a single wistful glance towards the Abbot's lavish table.

A WEDDING

THE OUTLAWS barely recognised their master when he appeared early the following day. Robin was dressed in the costume of a jester, red and yellow from head to foot. When he walked, the bells on his hat jingled. Maid Marian wore the short tunic and round cap of a page, and some of the outlaws were dressed in the ragged finery of wandering players.

"I may play the fool," said Robin grimly, "but it is the Abbot who will end up looking foolish."

Reminded of their errand, the colourful band set off in silence. Fifty bowmen accompanied them, walking five hundred paces behind. A few miles from St Mary's Abbey, Maid Marian held up her hand. "Listen," she whispered, "can you hear something?" Through the trees came the clear sound of a man's voice.

"It's a sad song he's singing," said Will Scarlet; who wore the costume of a Turkish knight.

Then the singer came into view. He was a handsome young man with golden curls and an elfin look about him. In his hands he carried a lute which he plucked mournfully. Robin leapt forward, ringing the bells on his jester's stick. "A merry morning to you, sad sir," he said.

"It's not a merry morning at all!" said the young man. "For my heart is broken. Fair Ellen is marrying an old goat at St Mary's. And there's only one person who can help me, and I don't know where he is."

"Your heart is not broken," said Robin, "and fair Ellen is not going to marry an old goat. St Mary's Abbey is where we are going."

"What use is a band of rascally players," wailed the young man, "when I need Robin Hood?"

Robin bowed. "At your service," he said. The young man's eyes widened in amazement. Then Robin laughed and put his arm round the minstrel's shoulders. As they walked towards the abbey, the young man told Robin and Marian his story. His name was Alan a Dale, and he was a wandering minstrel who had fallen in love with fair Ellen two years earlier. He was still talking about his Ellen when the outlaws reached St Mary's.

"Hide yourself in the chapel gallery," Robin told Alan. "If all has gone well, you should find a friend there. Be quick before anyone sees you."

As Alan a Dale hurried off, the outlaws gathered outside the chapel. Much the Miller did cartwheels and Jack Smithy juggled with apples. No one took any notice of the players except the Abbot; who vowed to have them whipped after the wedding. He was at the head of the procession which entered the chapel, and he was dressed in a richly embroidered gown ordered specially for the occasion. He was followed by the monks, a downtrodden bunch of starvelings who seemed terrified of their Abbot. Next came the groom, a toothless old man who leant on a stick and plucked at his wispy beard. Last to enter the chapel was Ellen. She walked slowly, her face white, her eyes wide with horror. Villagers who had come to watch the wedding sighed at the thought of this fresh young girl marrying a man with one foot in the grave.

As Ellen walked up the aisle, two voices began to sing a psalm from the gallery. One was a rich bass, the other a fine tenor. Ellen started, but she did not look up. The Abbot tapped his foot in annoyance. As the psalm ended and the ceremony began, the door of the chapel burst open. The band of players tumbled in, skipping and cartwheeling up the aisle as if it were a fairground.

This was too much for the Abbot. "Stop!" he roared. "Cease this play-acting!"

"Just what I was going to say to you, Abbot," said Robin. "This is no more a proper wedding than we are proper players." With that he pulled a horn out of his jester's tunic and blew a blast on it. Fifty bowmen in Lincoln green rushed into the chapel.

"Now for a real wedding," shouted Robin. "Where is Ellen's true love?"

"I am here," shouted Alan a Dale from the gallery.

"But where is a priest to marry them?" snarled the Abbot. "No monk of mine would sink so low." He glared at the rows of wretched monks who shuffled their feet and looked at the ground.

"I am here," shouted a rich bass voice from the gallery.

"Brother Michael!" said the Abbot in disgust.

Then the fat friar came down from the gallery and performed the marriage. He said the words of the ceremony so loudly that even those waiting outside the chapel door could hear. In no time at all Alan a Dale and his fair Ellen were married. Then the band of players and the fifty green-clad bowmen and Brother Michael Tuck and the young couple made their way back to the greenwood to celebrate the wedding in Sherwood style.

Friar Tuck never mastered the art of the longbow, but food at the outlaws' camp improved considerably with his coming.

As for the Abbot and his monks and the tottering bridegroom, they remained locked in the chapel until well after nightfall.

THE SHERIFF'S SILVER

OF ALL ROBIN'S men Little John was the best loved. Children and animals followed him, and he was everyone's friend. There was only one person whom Little John hated. Many years ago the Sheriff of Nottingham had whipped a small boy for taking a log of firewood. Little John had been only nine years old then, but he still bore the scars.

Now he wanted to teach the Sheriff a lesson and he asked Robin for permission to go to Nottingham.

Robin frowned. "Be careful," he said, "I do not want to lose you."

"You will hear from me in a week," said Little John, "and this is what I want you to do." Then he outlined his plan to Robin and set off. He was too well-known a figure to pass unnoticed in Nottingham. The townspeople whispered and pointed at him, and soon he was surrounded by a band of armed men. Little John laughed and put down his staff.

"Tell your master I wish to speak to him," he said.

When the Sheriff saw the huge man standing before him, he rubbed his pudgy hands with glee. "So Robin Hood has a traitor in his midst," he chortled. "A turncoat."

Little John started forward with rage, but then he remembered why he had come. He bowed to the Sheriff. "I've come to offer you my services, sir. And," he bent down to whisper in the Sheriff's ear, "to help you capture Robin Hood."

The Sheriff licked his lips nervously. "Why should I trust you?" he asked.

Little John frowned. "Master Hood has decided to get rid of me," he said. "Master Hood said I was a drunken fool." He spoke quietly so that only the Sheriff could hear. "I wish to get even with Master Hood. That is why you can trust me, Lord Sheriff."

The Sheriff looked hard at Little John. The man seemed to have a genuine grievance. "How do you propose to catch him?" he asked.

"Let me prove myself first," said Little John, "and then I shall tell you."

The Sheriff was still uncertain. "I shall have you watched," he said.

"Like a hawk," agreed Little John.

"I could have you hanged," said the Sheriff.

"So you could," replied Little John, and he laughed

uproariously.

The Sheriff made up his mind. "You may help in the kitchen," he said and hurried off without waiting for an answer.

The kitchen was worse than Little John had ever imagined. For six long days he scoured pots and scrubbed floors. On the seventh day the Sheriff asked to see him. "Well, what of Sherwood?" he said impatiently.

Little John pretended not to understand. "I have heard, sir," he said, "that there is a mighty stag in the forest with over two hundred hind."

"I am not speaking of deer," the Sheriff said crossly. "What about Robin Hood?"

"And I have also heard," Little John went on, "that Sir Guy is riding out to the forest the day after tomorrow."

At the mention of Sir Guy's name, the Sheriff leant forward. He could not bear the thought that Sir Guy might take the huge stag. "Gisborne is overstepping the mark," he muttered, and he forgot all about Robin Hood.

"We shall go hunting tomorrow!" he announced. Then he added, "You are a good fellow, Little John, but I think I shall leave you behind."

"Very wise, sir," said Little John. His plan was going well.

The hunting party left early. Little John made short work of the soldier who was put in charge of him. He tripped him up and locked him in the cellar. The cook was more difficult. He was a good swordsman and determined to defend the buttery where the Sheriff kept his silver. But he was no match for Little John who picked up a broom and sent the sword flying out of the window. As the cook attempted to follow his sword, Little John seized him. "I have work for you, my friend," he said.

The cook trembled as he saw Little John empty the Sheriff's silver into two sacks – dishes, bowls, plates, goblets and candlesticks. "Now for the greenwood," said Little John, "and you are coming with me!" Then he heaved one of the sacks on to the cook's back, and the two set off round the back streets in the direction of Sherwood.

The Sheriff's hunting party rode round the forest for hours. They saw no sign of the miraculous stag, but the Sheriff was prepared to wait. As he rode into a large clearing, he caught a glimpse of a magnificent pair of antlers. Then an owl hooted, and another. A horn blew and men began to pour out of the forest. Some dropped from branches, some crawled from bramble thickets, some came from behind fallen trees. There must have been more than two hundred of them, all dressed in green.

Last of all came Robin wearing a huge pair of antlers on his head. He smiled merrily at the Sheriff. "So you have found your mighty stag at last!" he said. Then he bowed low so that the antlers scraped the ground. "Our camp is quite close," Robin continued, "and you are invited to dine with us there. A new experience for you, Sheriff. What do you say?"

The Sheriff said nothing. He watched silently as his men and horses were sent on their way back to Nottingham. Then he put on the faded suit of Lincoln green which Jack Smithy handed him. Without his silks and furs, the little man looked a sorry sight. He was not used to walking, and he arrived at the outlaws' camp quite exhausted.

"We'll make an outlaw of you yet!" shouted Robin. "Sit down and eat, Master Sheriff."

The sturdy oak tables gleamed with silver dishes. Robin blew his horn, and food was brought out. The Sheriff watched in amazement as Little John set down a dish in front of him – Little John whom he had that morning left at the castle under guard. He had been well and truly tricked.

"Do you like our silver, Sheriff?" roared Little John.

"Robbed from some poor traveller, no doubt," muttered the Sheriff.

"Look closer, Sheriff," said Little John.

Then the Sheriff saw that it was his own silver on the table. His white face turned red with rage.

"You have not tasted our fine food," said Little John and he clapped his hands. A shamefaced cook came

forward and bowed. "Your own silver and your own cook," said Little John. "We wanted to make you feel at home!"

The Sheriff was speechless with fury. He ate nothing and sat silently while the outlaws feasted. Finally Little John stood up. "A night in the greenwood is what our Sheriff needs. Then he will be a true outlaw."

The Sheriff did not sleep at all well. His head was under a holly bush, and a great oak root dug into his back. When dawn came, his limbs were so stiff he could not move. Two outlaws pulled him to his feet.

"Now for a tour of the forest before we send you home," said Little John.

It was evening when the Sheriff stumbled into Nottingham. His green doublet was covered in mud and he smelled of pond water. People turned aside as he passed and dogs barked at him. No one recognised him. His face was so covered in bramble scratches that his own gatekeeper turned him away. He had to go round to the back of the castle and creep in through the kennels.

After a bath and a change of clothes, the Sheriff summoned Sir Guy of Gisborne. The two sat talking far into the night until at last Sir Guy came up with a plan to trap Robin Hood once and for all.

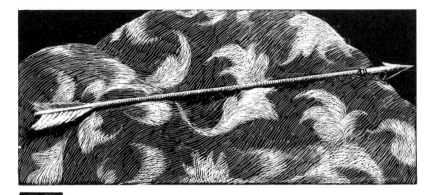

THE GOLDEN ARROW

MUCH THE MILLER brought news of the Sheriff's contest. "There's an arrow made of solid gold for the winner," he said. "Robin is sure to win it."

"Robin must win it," growled Little John.

But when the archers lined up in front of the target, Robin was not among them. The Sheriff was bitterly disappointed. His plan had failed. And Sir Guy had been so certain that Robin would take up the challenge. The Sheriff walked up and down the row of bowmen, peering into each face in turn. One man had grey eyes, but he was a small, stocky fellow. The others were all professional soldiers; except for a curly-haired boy who stood at the end of the line.

Sir Guy of Gisborne stood apart. He was too proud to join the contestants, but he, like them, carried a bow.

As the last man was counted, a figure limped up to the Sheriff. He was a stooped old man who wore the scarred leather apron of a cobbler. The curly-haired boy rushed to his side. "Grandfather, I told you to stay at home." The boy turned to the Sheriff. "He would insist on coming, my lord."

"May not a cobbler shoot as well as a knight?" asked the old man in a quavering voice.

"He may," sneered Sir Guy, "if he can. Come, Sheriff, let us begin this ridiculous contest."

The Sheriff gave the signal, and two trumpeters sounded a fanfare. Prince John's standard was raised. "God bless our noble Prince," shouted Sir Guy. There was a ragged chorus of support. Then one of the bowmen cried out, "And God bless the true King." The Sheriff whipped round to see who had spoken, but by now everyone was shouting for the King. The Sheriff hurriedly held up his glove. "Let the contest begin," he shouted and dropped the glove.

One of the soldiers was first to shoot. He sent his arrow flying straight for the bull's-eye. Sir Guy's shot landed so close that the soldier's arrow fell out of the target and dropped to the ground.

The boy shot next, but his arrow was wide of the mark. The other arrows were close to Sir Guy's, but not close enough. When the last man had shot, the old cobbler turned to his grandson. "Lend me your bow, lad," he said. "Let me try my luck." The boy handed him the bow. No one noticed its tarnished silver tips. The cobbler drew back the string and let fly. No one afterwards could say exactly what happened next. One moment the old man's arrow was speeding through the air, and the next it stuck quivering in the bull's-eye and Sir Guy's arrow lay on the ground, split clean in half.

"The best of three shots, Sheriff, is it not?" snapped Sir Guy.

"I expect so," said the Sheriff. He was looking intently at the old cobbler. All he could see was a mild-faced old man with grey eyes, a long beard and a limp.

The soldier, the cobbler, and Sir Guy shot again. All three arrows landed in the red circle round the bull's-eye. "Wake up," shouted someone in the crowd. The Sheriff knew that voice – he would never forget it. It was Little John! So the outlaws had come to the contest after all. The Sheriff looked into the crowd. Then he whispered something to Sir Guy.

The contest had reached the last round. This time the old cobbler shot first. A roar went up from the crowd as his arrow landed dead in the centre of the target. The soldier's arrow landed on the outer edge of the bull's-eye. Then Sir Guy drew his bow. At the last possible moment he turned and suddenly shot into the crowd, seemingly at random. A huge man fell to the ground with an arrow buried in the flesh of his thigh.

"Little John!" gasped someone as the cloak fell back to reveal the man's yellow hair.

"Seize the cobbler," shrieked the Sheriff, but while all eyes were on the crowd, the old man had snatched up the hand of his grandson and the two had slipped away.

The golden arrow lay forgotten on its silken cushion.

OLD ENEMIES

SIR GUY HAD seen a look pass between the old man and the curly-haired boy. And in that moment he realised who they were: the youth with the black curls was Lady Marian Fitzwalter. And that meant that the limping cobbler must be...

"A change of plan," he shouted and caught hold of the Sheriff's padded sleeve. "We must leave this rabble and go to Sherwood. Robin Hood will not dare attack while we have Little John captive."

The Sheriff's little eyes turned away from Sir Guy's piercing glance. After his experience in the forest he had sworn never to go within a mile of Sherwood ever again. Then came Sir Guy's mocking voice.

"Surely my Lord Sheriff cannot be afraid?"

The Sheriff stiffened. He saw Little John struggling to get up. "Yes," he said slowly. "You are right: perhaps we should go hunting in the forest. And take this wounded giant to be our bait."

Within an hour, the Sheriff and fifty horsemen rode out of Nottingham. They looked as if they were going into battle. The Sheriff wore a helmet with plumes and a kitchen maid asked if there was going to be a tournament. Then she caught sight of Sir Guy of Gisborne and said no more. Sir Guy was wrapped in a cape made of stiff black horsehide. A helmet hid his face, but in his eyes there was a look of death.

Little John limped after the horsemen. He had been tied up in knots like a pudding, but he managed to wink at the townspeople as he passed. On the outskirts of Sherwood, Sir Guy stopped. "I know you do not care for the forest, Sheriff," he said. "Let me meet Robin Hood alone. I am curious to come face to face with the villain at last. I shall sound my horn when he is dead."

The Sheriff was only too pleased to stay behind with Little John and the soldiers, and Sir Guy went into the forest alone. He soon found his quarry. Robin had taken off his disguise and was leaning against the trunk of an old ash tree, waiting for him.

"Robin Hood," shouted Sir Guy, "I have come to kill Robin Hood."

Robin walked towards Sir Guy. "Is it Robin Hood you seek or...?" he left the question unfinished.

Sir Guy looked into Robin's face. "We are old enemies," said Robin calmly.

"Robert Locksley!" said Sir Guy between gritted teeth. "I might have guessed that you were not dead."

He slid off his horse and the two men drew their swords. Sir Guy fought like a madman. Robin needed all his skill to defend himself. Again and again he struck at Sir Guy's horsehide cape, but the hide was as hard as iron and Robin's sword barely dented its polished surface.

Then suddenly it was over. Maddened by the look of pity in his opponent's eyes, Sir Guy took a lunge at Robin's head. And in that moment, Robin's sword found a gap in the horsehide cape. Sir Guy fell lifeless to the ground.

"It was kill or be killed," said Robin soberly. He knelt down and unfastened the hunting horn from Sir Guy's belt. Then he carefully removed the cape and helmet, put them on and blew the horn.

On the edge of the forest, the Sheriff heard the sound of the horn. "A kill, a kill!" he shouted gleefully, and he cantered into the forest, leaving his men to follow with Little John.

The Sheriff was not the only person to hear the horn. Maid Marian had gone ahead to tell Will Scarlet of Little John's capture. Now he and a band of anxious outlaws emerged from the cover of the trees. Robin told them to stand guard round the clearing. "But do not show yourselves," he said. "We cannot put Little John's life in danger. I must meet the Sheriff alone."

Wrapped in Sir Guy's horsehide cape, with his helmet pulled well down, Robin waited. Soon the Sheriff appeared. "At last, my friend," he wheezed, "at last the villain is dead."

Robin said nothing. He watched the Sheriff dismount and waited until he had reached Sir Guy's body. Then he pulled the Sheriff's arm behind his back and held a knife to his ribs.

"Yes, Sheriff, you are right!" said Robin. "The villain is dead." He took off the helmet and threw the horsehide cape on the ground.

The Sheriff's face crumpled. He could not breathe. "Robin Hood!" he choked out. Then Will Scarlet and his men came forward and the Sheriff began to tremble. "Don't kill me, don't kill me," he moaned.

"Where is Little John?" asked Robin sternly.

"He isn't here," cried the Sheriff. "My soldiers have him." At that moment there was a sound of scuffling in the bushes. "Free the prisoner," shrieked the Sheriff. "Let him go free. Quickly!" He was almost sobbing with fright. Then Little John's huge figure lumbered up to the ash tree. He was limping badly now and his tunic was soaked with blood. He was followed by two soldiers—one of them had a swollen eye and the other seemed hardly able to walk. Robin hugged Little John.

"I see you have left your mark, old friend," he said. "Now you must think what we should do with this

stuffed pigeon. It is for you to decide."

Little John looked down at the Sheriff. "I wouldn't stain my sword with his blood," he said. "Death is too good for him. What he needs is a good whipping. Remember young John Little who got whipped for stealing a log, Sheriff?"

The Sheriff was not listening. "Don't kill me," he whimpered. "I'll do anything for you, anything at all."

"Just remove your fat little person from our forest," said Little John. "And take this with my good wishes." Wincing with pain, Little John gave the Sheriff a great kick with his good leg. Then he and Robin and the rest of the outlaws vanished into the forest.

The Sheriff and his men made their weary way back to Nottingham, carrying Sir Guy's body. Sir Guy was buried in the vault at Gisborne castle, and no one mourned his death for long.

THE TALL PILGRIM

AFTER THE DEATH of Sir Guy of Gisborne, Robin and his men led a quieter life. Occasionally an unwary merchant or wealthy bishop might be ambushed in the forest. Once or twice a year Friar Tuck led a raid on the pantry and cellars of St Mary's Abbey. And Little John went on thinking up schemes for upsetting the Sheriff. Robin took to walking alone in the forest.

There was no news of the King. Some said he was in prison in Austria, others that he had died in the Holy Land. Meanwhile England suffered under the rule of Prince John and such men as the Sheriff. Sometimes Robin felt that Sherwood was the only peaceful place left in the kingdom.

It was while he was out walking one day that a tall stranger suddenly appeared at his side. He wore the wide hat of a pilgrim and he carried a staff.

"I seek Robin Hood of Sherwood," said the tall pilgrim.

"I hear he shoots the King's deer."

"For food, not for sport, like some," said Robin.

"I hear he disobeys the King's laws."

"Not the true King's laws," said Robin, "only cruel edicts made by that cut-throat brother of his."

"I hear he annoys the Sheriff."

"Yes," said Robin bitterly, "by freeing children from the gallows."

"I should like to meet the man," said the tall pilgrim.

"In that case," said Robin, "you shall, for I am Robin Hood." Then he invited the tall pilgrim to dine, and led the way to the outlaws' camp. There was something about the pilgrim that Robin could not understand. He had the calm serious manner of a holy man, but he carried himself like a man of action. The wide hat was pulled well down and Robin could not see his face.

The pilgrim ate and drank and laughed with the outlaws. The lines round his mouth deepened when he heard Robin and Marian speak of the cruel Sheriff and the greedy Abbot and proud Sir Guy of Gisborne.

After the meal, Alan a Dale sang and then the outlaws called for an archery contest. A garland of twigs was nailed to a dead oak tree.

Jack Smithy was in high spirits. "Anyone who misses the garland gets the knock from Robin," he shouted. The outlaws roared with delight. They lined up and solemnly took aim. Every arrow but one stuck fast in the garland.

Friar Tuck was busy with a half-eaten pie and his arrow missed the tree altogether.

"Friar Tuck for the knock," shouted the outlaws, and Robin gave the fat friar a friendly cuff. The tall pilgrim watched in silence.

Then the outlaws prepared to shoot at the willow wand in the centre of the garland. Everyone had three turns, and they all missed except Maid Marian and Will Scarlet, who hit the wand but did not split it. The men received their knocks amiably enough, and then the quiet stranger spoke: "Does your leader not take part in the contest?"

"No point," said Little John. "He always wins."

The pilgrim turned to Robin. "There is talk of your skill with the bow up and down the land," he said. "I should like to see it with my own eyes."

Robin could not refuse. He picked up his silver-tipped bow, aimed quickly at the wand and split it in two. Another wand was cut and stripped. That one, too, Robin's arrow split clean in half. A third was fetched and Robin drew back his bow. At his side the pilgrim leant forward eagerly and a shaft of sunlight lit up his face. Robin glimpsed the strong straight nose, the broad brow, and a pair of piercing blue eyes and his aim faltered momentarily. The arrow buried itself in the garland round the wand.

"Robin for the knock," shouted the outlaws.

"I shall give the knock," said the tall pilgrim imperiously. He stood up and with one blow he felled Robin to the ground. As the men rushed forward, the pilgrim took off his hat. Little John fell to his knees, and the others followed.

"King Richard!" said Robin. "At last you have come home."

"I wanted to see Robin Hood for myself," said the King.

"But Sire, you should not have come alone," said Robin; as the King helped him up.

"Oh, I did not come alone," said the King and he held up his hand. At once a hundred crossbowmen surrounded the camp.

"Tricked on our own doorstep!" said Little John in disgust.

King Richard laughed. "I have come to punish you, not to take you prisoner."

Robin knelt down in front of the King. "We have killed, Sire, but only in self-defence. We have stolen from the rich, but only to give to the poor. And we have tried to right wrongs and fight injustice."

"Rise Robert Locksley, also called Robin Hood of Sherwood," said the King. "I pardon you and all your followers on one condition."

"What is it, Sire?" asked Robin.

"That you and Maid Marian and fifty of your best archers accompany me to London. My bowmen have no

skill in the longbow, and they need teaching."

"My thanks, Sire," said Robin and he bowed his head.

"And as for that lying, thieving puffball who calls himself a Sheriff," said the King, "he shall be punished!"

"And I say hurrah to that," shouted Little John, beaming with delight.

THE LAST ARROW

TO LITTLE JOHN'S lasting joy, the Sheriff of Nottingham was disgraced. His chain of office was torn from his shoulders and he was put in the stocks for everyone to laugh at. Robin and Marian and fifty men rode with the King to London and instructed the royal bowmen in the use of the longbow.

In time they wearied of the sights and smells of the city. They longed for the huge oaks and dappled sunlight of the forest. Within a few months they were all back in Sherwood, and there they lived for the rest of their lives.

As the years passed, Friar Tuck grew fatter and fatter, and Little John's yellow mane turned quite white. Then early one spring Maid Marian caught a fever and died. Robin was heartbroken. His aim was as true as before, and his courage as keen, but the laughter had gone out of his grey eyes. He felt old and ill and weary of life.

To the north of Sherwood lay a priory which was

famous for its skill in healing. There Robin went, taking with him Little John for company. The Prioress was a striking woman, narrow-faced and cold-voiced. She examined Robin and pronounced that he had a fever: his blood was thick and needed letting. Little John waited outside the priory while Robin was taken to one of the little cells the nuns used for private prayer.

The Prioress was quick and efficient with her work, and soon Robin knew that she would bind up his arm and let him sleep. But the Prioress did not bind his arm. She stood by the door of the little room, and spoke softly. "I had a nephew once. His name was Guy and he died many years ago. Now his murderer lies before me with his lifeblood running out." Robin realised that he had been trapped for the last time. Sir Guy of Gisborne had been avenged.

Too weak to rise from his bed, he lifted his horn and blew three times. Soon he heard Little John shouting, and then the big man was in the room, pushing the Prioress out of the way.

"Lift me up, Little John," Robin said, "so I may see the forest." Little John raised his master so that he could look out of the narrow window.

"I am dying, Little John," said Robin.

Little John made no answer, but the tears ran down his cheeks. "Hand me my bow," Robin whispered.

With the last of his strength Robin drew the bow and

shot. The arrow sped across the priory garden and into the field, reaching a huge oak tree which marked the beginning of the forest. "Bury me where the arrow fell," Robin said and died.

No stone marked Robin's grave under the huge oak, but Little John planted daffodils and bluebells there. Squirrels came to search for acorns and deer kept the grass cropped short. "The last piece of Sherwood," Little John told his grandson years later.

But the little boy did not want to hear that part of the story. "Tell it again, grandfather," he said, "right from the beginning, from the time you first met Robin and pushed him in the river."